PUNS

A Collection of Puns, Dad Jokes, Bad Jokes, and Wordplay

Kevin Kelleher
Lucas Kelleher
Michael Kelleher
Stephen Kelleher

Illustrations by Lucas Kelleher

Contributing Punsmiths:

Pete Baker
Mason Beets
Sean Coughlin
Gary DeWitt
Connie E. Driscoll
Darren Driscoll

Adam Fritz
Deb Kelleher
Patrick Kelleher
Eduardo Lopez
Jon Rodriguez
Erin Zelnio

First Printing, 2024

ISBN: 9798320441948
Published by Ahmnition
www.ahmnition.com

Printed in the United States of America

Cover Art & Illustrations by Lucas Kelleher
www.kelleherbros.com

Design & Layout by Laura McBride
www.lauramcbride.com

For the dads

Table of Contents

IntroPUNction

The pun is an exacting art form, combining poetic craft with a sense of humor. A good pun hinges on the inherent similarity of two words or sounds, yet the door that swings upon those hinges can open the way to a surprisingly deep insight, to a belly-laugh, or even to a groan of psychic pain.

Such is the power of the pun.

Stephen Kelleher, the father of five boys, started recording his best puns in the family round robin letter exchanged amongst his siblings. After a few decades, the puns started piling up.

Stephen's predilection for word-humor was passed onto all five sons, but three of them also started keeping track of their jokes over the years: Lucas, Michael, and Kevin.

Lucas and Kevin even put together their own long lists of puns for publication online, Lucas having set up an automated posting for Legendary Puns on Twitter which posted a pun each day for more than a year.

With all these great puns just lying around, something needed to be done with them. Behold! That something is what you now hold in your hands: the very best of the work of four talented punsmiths, hand selected from more than half a century of combined toil.

PUNfection includes our most perfect puns – their meaning can be interpreted in at least two different ways, and more than one way works within the context of the joke. Either that, or they are just plain clever or funny enough to warrant top billing.

ComeupPUNs is the next tier, made of puns which are either funny or clever (sometimes both), but which don't typically confuse more than one meaning.

PUNishment is there for our true humor masochists. These jokes are bad. They are shameful. By including them in this book, we are helping to make the world a worse place. You should probably avoid Part Three, if you can help it.

Finally, *Pun Runs* compiles lists of related puns into longer-running joke-streams.

Enjoy! ...If you dare.

-The Kellehers

Part One:

PUNfection

1. Choo-Choo Ka-Ching

During the great train boom, I sold so many rails it was hard to keep track.

2. Digging Deep

R&D is working on a new shovel design, and this is really groundbreaking research.

3. Getting Your Money's Worth

Self-driving cars may be expensive, but at least you have something to chauffer it.

4. Layout at the Pool

Where's the diving board usually situated? Well, at deep ends.

5. Well, Which Is It?

If the choice is between climbing rungs or just giving up, I choose the ladder.

6. The Direct Approach

An art thief went into a museum and asked if he could take some pictures.

7. Sew Obviously in Stitches

The tailor may appear to be a knit-wit, but there's more to her than their seams.

8. Marine Biologist

After a particularly bad date, the marine biologist refocused herself on her cataloguing work. After all, she reminded herself, there are plenty of fish indices.

9. Librarians Be Warned

The Dewey Decimal System is to be used only as a last re-sort.

10. Guilty as Tin

Did you hear about the tin factory employees caught having sex with foodstuffs? Authorities say they're doing everything they can.

11. Happy Birthday

My girlfriend Edith threatened to dump me on my birthday if I gain another pound, so now I can't have my cake and Edith too.

12. Common Cents

Mobsters had for years improvised a weapon of a sock filled with quarters, but even when they tried to discontinue its use, they had to contend with the fact that change is hard.

13. Antisocial Eel

Introverted eels can become antisocial if
they're not good with social morays.

14. The Spice of Life

Our pizza chef used to be in the military. Sometimes his hands will shake at work and he'll spill oregano all over himself, so I suppose he's a seasoned veteran.

15. Top Brass

Regulators are anxious to establish import guidelines for copper/zinc metal alloys. They really want to get down to brass tax.

16. Fat Chance

If you don't understand how to prepare butter, allow me to clarify.

17. The Daring Butcher

Making sausage takes guts.

18. Ill Omen

Whenever I can't recognize my own signature I think, "Oh, that's a bad sign...."

19. Busy Librarians

Librarians have hardly any free time because their schedules are all booked up.

20. Resident Resentment

Two lab technicians sat directly across from one another inspecting blood samples for expiration, but they never spoke a word. There was too much bad blood between them.

21. Poetry is Hard

Amateur poets need not apply – leave it to the prose.

22. It's a Cinch

This new Easy Clasp buckle design is truly fasten-aiding.

23. Less for Success

If you are trying to get your toddler off the bottle, some slowly lower the amount in the bottle gradually until they finally remove it all together. It's a weaning strategy.

24. Sad Truth

Has an underage prostitute lost something? In a sense.

25. English Professor

Between drinking, driving, and crashing, the English professor could not avoid an Oxford coma.

26. Deviant Delights

If you're into sodomy with mining tools, then I've got a pick to bone with you.

27. Livestock Inventory

The farmer who used to take inventory of his livestock at random has decided to do it in a specific order, hens-fourth.

28. Church Music

When church cantors get lazy planning music for mass, a lot can be left to chants.

29. Paddle to the Metal

There was a sports shop which was having a sale on oversize canoe oars. To canoe owners, this was an excellent deal, but to the salesman it was a huge oar deal.

30. Pretense

The platform built to test out the initial fake campsite was put up under false pre-tents.

31. Cider Bartering

The cider brewery used to barter with orchards for flavors before they were busted for in-cider trading. All it takes is a few bad apples....

32. Love At First Sleight

The only criminal to ever steal my heart was an organ trafficker.

33. Sales Tactic

Any jewelry salesman knows a customer is more likely to buy a custom brooch if they can see what it looks like while they're wearing it first, but it's up to them to find a way to brooch the subject.

34. Personal Style

I would wear a straight jacket, but I'm not sure I can pull it off.

35. Swine and Dine

A man was paid to cater a barbecue pork meal, but he secretly substituted some donkey meat. After the host bit into the donkey meat, he really chewed ass.

36. Jogging Coach

I've had no luck finding a good jogging coach. Everyone just keeps giving me the runaround.

37. Picky Eaters

People who won't accept cannibalism lying down have to be fed up.

38. The Old Dam

If you could spruce up the old hydroelectric dam with new gates and fresh paint, it would make you feel good – pretty-dam good.

39. In Creased Output

Origami should be practiced in a folding chair.

40. See Food

I can't eat at restaurants that are too dimly lit, because they never serve my salad the way I like it: a little light on the dressing.

41. Burrito in a Haystack

I can't find burritos anywhere on the menu. Maybe they're keeping it under "Wraps".

42. Man Up

Castration takes balls.

43. His & Hers Claus

Those who doubt if Santa Claus can really visit every household in a single night often accuse Mrs. Claus of helping, but of course that's a classic case of he sled, she sled.

44. Family Gathering

After spending the holidays accurately measuring the height of all my relatives, I just can't taller rate them anymore.

45. Finding a Solution

If you think you can lower the ratio of certain particles within your own body, then you're only diluting yourself.

46. Positively Negative

I was asked why my comments, in general, seem often to be so critical. I could only reply, "I'm not positive."

47. All's Fair

Both bakeries were lost to fire after two bakers sabotaged each other's equipment. Eventually they would make up, since all's flarin' oven war.

48. Apotheosis

If I could just transform myself into a god, I'd be Set for life!

49. Turntable Techniques

After an exhaustive search for the best DJs and turntable techniques, we had still only just scratched the surface.

50. Historical Accuracy

Birth control is forbidden at the Renaissance Fair – to keep things authentic for the period.

51. Ice Cold

There was a member of the Olympic luge team who was unusually tall for that sport. He had trouble getting dates because he was a big luge'r.

52. Emissions Testing

Emissions testing is exhausting work.

53. Old Habits

Those nuns use the dye from their worn out clothes to color all of their sheep black. I've asked them to stop, but old habits dye herd, I guess.

54. Like Clockwork

After taking a lot of time off, the pendulum maker found it difficult getting back into the swing of things.

55. RBG

Ever since the passing of Justice Ginsberg, the Supreme Court has been utterly Ruth-less.

56. Body Modification

I'm trying to decide how big to stretch out the hole in my earlobe, but it's something that's really hard to gauge.

57. R.I.P.

I'll never forget my grandfather's last words before he finally kicked the bucket... "I hate this damned bucket!"

58. Physics Research Tower

Placing the "Attraction Force of Physical Bodies Department" in the basement gave the physics building a low Center of Gravity.

59. Stigma

A defect in the spherical curvature of the eye shouldn't affect how others treat you, and yet there's definitely astigmatism there.

60. Grandfather Clock

If anything happens to that grandfather clock, you're gonna owe me big time.

61. Lit Lit.

A poet had a routine in which she would take an early bath after supper and then spend a few hours writing. She would have scented candles lighted for inspiration as she bathed, but one day she discovered that she only had one candle left. The atmosphere was not right and her poetry did not come easily that night. She was down to her last scent, and her evening had gone from bath to verse.

62. Type-O

Of writers who sit down and open a vein on the page, the most versatile among them are typo negative.

63. Shopping List

I have to write down what I need beforehand, or otherwise I'll just wander around the grocery store listlessly.

64. Ikea Captive

Everytime I'm in an Ikea I feel like a captive, but I keep coming back for more decor. Maybe I have stock-home syndrome.

65. Pants on Fire

Any monk who sings embellishments on a harp about how they prefer wearing trousers to traditional robes is a lyre liar pants-on friar.

66. Gone South

Two boys were given a project to make a map, but when the first started drawing it sideways, the second said, "You're doing it wrong! You've got North on the right hand side, but North should be at the top." "I always draw my maps this way," the first boy replied, carrying on. The second boy threw down his pencil and said, "Fine, then finish it without me. The West is up to you."

67. Sword of Nice

There is a sword and knife dealer who gets overwhelmed once every sword in his shop is spoken for. Try not to bother him when that happens, as he is more than slightly out of swords.

68. Playing in the Dark Room

I've been playing a game with old photographs for hours. It's still fun!

69. Keeping Up

In an ongoing effort to clean up the waterfront, the city has been keeping up with a-pier rinses.

70. Hifalutin

The skydiving burglar carried himself with an air of assumed importance. He was certainly high-fall lootin'.

71. I Don't Believe It

People mourning the loss of someone they didn't know is un-bereavable.

72. Frenchmen in Turbans

Whenever I see three Frenchmen in turbans, I think, *Très sheik!*

73. Bulky Booty

A pill to enlarge my glutes is an idea that I can really get behind. But it'd better work on both cheeks equally; I don't want to do it half-assed.

74. Failure en Math

One football team had the worst statistics of any defense in the league. They had the worst average against the run and the worst average against the pass, as well as the overall worst average points scored against them. One of the linemen was trying to explain the poor statistics, but it was not going well; it was a case of the end justifying the means.

75. An Ice Gesture

A cryogenic scientist was able to teach a rat how to solve math equations, but wanted to know if those math skills would be affected by the process of freezing and thawing. So she froze her intelligent rat and began teaching a second one. By accident, the first rat was left out of the freezer and thawed, and when the scientist returned, the two rats had gotten mixed up. Dismayed, the scientist offered her lab technician a raise if he could determine which rat was which. The technician said he didn't need a raise, but "It's the thawed that counts."

76. The Naked Truth

The owner of an art gallery had declining sales. He thought he could increase traffic in the gallery if he featured more high-quality paintings with nudity. With his business teetering on the verge of bankruptcy, he really needed some good nudes.

77. Can I Pick Your Brain?

Bought a pithing needle last week. I'm bored with it now.

78. Beer & Comedy Festival

Did you hear about the controversy surrounding the Craft Beer & Comedy festival? It was a real brew-ha-ha.

79. Sphere Joy

My favorite possession as a kid was this old, beat up, outdated globe. It still had the USSR on it, but it meant the world to me.

80. Vinyl

You're telling me you've got the first-ever vinyl disk to be inscribed with a spiral groove? Well, that's gotta be some kind of record!

81. Band Together

I'm hoping to start a collection of mallet percussion instruments. Everyone send me good vibes!

82. Under the Big Top

Circus band members used to travel between gigs, going from one to the next, but ever since they switched to electronic music, those jobs have been taken over by circuits musicians.

83. The Ol' Switcheroo

Remember when you asked for a pun
and I built you a doorframe instead? You
totally walked into that one!

84. Propaganda

Always configure your propaganda with a pair of misleading images, so it's easy: two visual lies.

85. Cowardly Archer

What does the cowardly archer do with their arrows? A little quiver in the corner.

86. Viticulture

The Horn of Africa must be a great place to study wine, because so many Somali A's come from there.

87. Lion's Trim

The zoo gets the lion's share of its publicity from the new animal hair stylist. The big cats' routine trim is now the mane event.

88. Confessions

As a cereal monogamist, I was happy with the same thing every day. Well, except for the occasional Trix on the side.

89. Fired Barista

The barista was fired for allowing grinds to make it into the brew pot. That kind of negligence was grounds for dismissal.

90. Powers That Be

Before I can begin my study of melittology, I'll need to get approval from the powers that bee.

91. Hearts Aflame

The kindling never felt a burning desire for anything until he met his match.

92. Context is Everything

Leaving your glasses at home might not make sense, out of contacts.

93. Lights Out

We could try turning out the lights before the injection to see if it will hurt any less, but it's a shot in the dark.

94. Pufferfish

The pufferfish contains a deadly toxin, and any undercooked fish can have salmonella, so you've really got to pick your *poisson*.

95. Giving the Slip

I accidentally brought up my wife's psychiatry-themed undergarment in conversation – a real Freudian slip.

96. Intellectual Property

This Canadian microbrewery keeps tight control over their hoppy brand & trademarks. They're very protective of their IP, eh?

97. Bar Tops

Tavern connoisseurs are mesmerized by old wood countertops, but hate trendy new materials. So if it ain't bar-oak, don't fixate.

98. Satan & Tennis

For centuries, Satan had lured impressionable young athletes to financial ruin by betting with him on games of tennis. But when the clamoring of angry souls in hell got to be too loud, he finally quit that infernal racket.

Part Two:

ComeupPUNs

99. A Friend in Need

Everyone likes lending money to me because my debts are outstanding!

100. You Might've Heard of Them

The place where I get my vinyl LPs is rather famous. They hold quite a few records, in fact.

101. Big Ask

You want me to collect a hundred EZ passes? That's one toll hoarder!

102. Flowery Language

Most modern species of flowers are bred only for their bright colors and many have no smell at all. The practice of bringing flowers to funerals was originally to cover the smell of the decaying body. Nowadays the new varieties may be pretty, but these flowers make no scents.

103. Quartz Countertops

When choosing a surface material for your countertops, quartz is really fantastic. But it's often taken for granite.

104. Whew!

While donating some old shirts, I nearly gave away my entire wardrobe. That was a clothes cull!

105. Class Was History

One day we had four students missing from a World History class, so I decided that with so many missing, we would not cover any new material that day. It was a four-gone conclusion.

106. Tolerance

To boost efficiency, the amusement park started charging an extra ticket price to anyone over six feet. That way, their rides could taller-rate more customers.

107. Ship Shaping Up

To all the authors who don't know how to write about the back of a boat, I'll have stern words for you – aft-towards.

108. Angry Sailor

A sailor was having problems raising the anchor; he lost control and gouged the deck when it came over the rail. He became very upset, having a history of problems with anchor management.

109. Good Things Come

If you visit the pond often enough to one day discover a $20 bill floating on the water, you will see that some things are worth wading for.

110. Lost Trailer

The truck drove away, leaving its trailer
behind. Although not the original plan,
everything went off without a hitch.

111. Simple Misunderstanding

Whenever I don't understand grammar, I just ask her to speak up.

112. Saw Expert

Though he has a bad temper, no one knows more about using a saw than Isnerio, making him a spicy Italian saw-sage.

113. No Problem

A self-spading cat is the kind of problem that fixes itself.

114. The Try in Carpentry

I should build a new shelf for all my books, but that would be a major project and I lack the shelf confidence.

115. Most Impressive

I do this impersonation of Monet falling into a printing press that always leaves quite the impression.

116. Called Out

My shiny new phone was giving me an inflated sense of self-importance, until someone called me on it.

117. Listen to Your Gut

At the Colon Workshop, my presentation on long-term constipation left quite an impact.

118. Car Rental Care

Leasing a new car is cheaper than buying one, so if I decide to provide a car to one of my children, it's the lease that I can do.

119. Data Sink

Whenever I think about how all my data is spread around multiple devices, I get a syncing feeling.

120. Hurry Up and Wait

I can have a joke ready in a gif, but it'll take me forever.

121. The Tops

The cabinet maker had to outsource jobs for custom kitchen countertops, because their own attempts proved to be counterproductive.

122. Catch 22

If the breeze dies while you're out on a rented sailboat, you've only got two options: wait maybe hours for the wind to return, or start slowly paddling, and risk returning the boat late. Either way, it's a no wind situation.

123. A Bird in Flight

Vultures take longer to start flying because they always have to check their carrion.

124. Vital Viticulture

Science allows us to graft old vines onto new ones. I know this will come as a grape re-leaf to you.

125. You've Got Male

Men can be especially defensive online if they feel they've been e-masculated.

126. A Good Match

Before convicted criminals take on professional wrestlers in the ring, someone has to weigh the Pros and Cons.

127. Gotta Give 'Em Credit

A local bank was family owned and staffed by three sisters: Denise was Vice President, Donna the Loan Officer, and Danielle a teller. They were very tough about giving credit. When you applied for a loan, Danielle gave you the application, Donna reviewed it, and Denise approved or denied it. If there was the slightest hint of credit problems, they cut you off at Denise.

128. Be Assertive

If you'd like to do business in Taiwan, it helps to have a Taipei personality.

129. Old Wounds

A medical grad student did her thesis on "Hard to Heal Wounds." Her husband never discussed the research or the thesis with her because it was a sore subject.

130. How May I Help You?

Actors who portray call service representatives can get by with just phoning it in.

131. Noble Birth

The idea that a king would sire a bastard is a common misconception.

132. Where the Rubber Meets the Road

If you're going to do exercises with massive tires, tread carefully. Though it can sure wear you down, I've been working out tirelessly for years.

133. Window Blinds

To shed some light on the effectiveness of various types of window coverings, a double blind study was needed.

134. Modern Art

You really should check out my atmospheric art installation entitled "Emphysema." ...It's breath-taking.

135. Beak Performance

A brief foray into aven dental care has left me at a floss for birds.

136. Box Office Potential

A film studio specialized in several types of genres and all of them did well except for mythological dramas. Every time they released a new movie, it was hit or myth.

137. Ramped Up

We've got the best ramps for sale here, if you're so inclined.

138. Medical Studies

I'd like to study the hemoglobic capacity of the brachial artery, or something in a similar vein.

139. Soap Opera

Somebody told me that farmers have a special soap for cleaning their pigs, but now I find out that it's just hogwash.

140. Laissez Faire

The county fair is in terrible shape thanks to the organizer's new "hands off" policy. They took a lazy fair approach.

141. This Time It's Personnel

Hiring a beautiful person to work for you would be a good business model.

142. Raven Mad

If a crow calls out to warn of danger, it's certainly caws for alarm.

143. Local Politics

If you say too many nice things about the landed gentry, angry peasants might make you dis a peer.

144. Rock and a Hard Place

Guitar players who can't figure out which effect boxes they need or which amplifier is best just have trouble making sound decisions.

145. European Banking

When your job is banking and lending in the EU, you've got to get paid what Euro'ed.

146. Wine Sleuth

When trying to identify mysterious wines, be sure you don't come to any bourgogne conclusions.

147. Lactose Intolerant

I felt bad for that server, having two prosthetic legs, when their customer sent back the cheese plate he brought them. But I suppose they must be lack-toes intolerant.

148. A Leg Up

Porpoises are sea mammals which
probably evolved from land mammals.
The fins of porpoises seem to have
developed from structures which would
have been legs and feet in their land
ancestors. In this case, evolution seems
to de-feet the porpoise.

149. Left Out in the Cold

If you know all about how people kept things cold before refrigerators... could use summer ice if forming?

150. Hauls Well

I attended a lecture about how to move furniture across the country, and I have to say it was a moving speech.

151. Hookah Lounge

Upon reflection, the hookah lounge's shiny new chrome decor was just smokin' mirrors.

152. Dark Humor

When the power's out, everything's free of charge.

153. Pushing the Envelope

Your editor deciding last minute that your article is too controversial is how you earn a "pull it" surprise.

154. Shoes Wisely

A shoe salesman got a good deal on a shipment of plus-sized shoes. It was hard work, but eventually he was able to sell every single one of them, and this was no small feet!

156. Shaking the Firm or Mint

Before they could put the safe in the moving van, it floated right up into the sky and disappeared into the clouds. If you think that God caused the safe to float away, that would be a safe assumption.

157. Time Sensitive

I urged the elderly clock repairman to exercise caution while he converted a used kitchen timer into a wristwatch. My exact words were, "Watch it, old timer!"

158. Grading on Curves

Despite high attendance at the school for fashion models, there are very few model students.

159. Just Riffing

When guitar soloists face-off on stage I demand my money back, because that's a total riff off.

159. Passionate Agrarians

A lot of farmers really love their soil, but I can't appreciate the sediment.

160. Ghost Writer

I'm going as a children's author for Halloween – Edward, I'll be.

161. Lonely at the Bottom

A church choir had four men, and three of them were tenors. Nobody knew just how good the bass was, though, as there was no basses for comparison.

162. Risqué Frisée

Inviting produce up to your apartment is one way to see how fresh it is.

163. Sculpting

You can shape clay with your hands sitting down, or chisel blocks of stone on a step stool, but a sculptor is either the former or the ladder.

164. Stereos

Since I'm biased, I'll keep my opinions on sound systems to myself to avoid stereotyping.

165. The Full Spectrum

Whenever I go anywhere faster than 671 million miles per hour, I always travel light.

166. Fare's Fair

Sneaking into the subway without paying for it is just no fare.

167. Gym Romance

Weightlifting Casanovas are always trying to pick up a bar Belle.

168. Dorian Decor

I was trying to find the right color of flowers for a Grecian temple, until I realized it would be un-Athena to our purple posies.

169. Yawn

Miners especially dislike drilling holes to hold dynamite. It's not only that working with explosives is dangerous, but drilling holes is just plain boring.

170. Slippery Slope

There's been utter chaos on the playground ever since the school got rid of all its slide rules.

171. Urbane Legend

A stage performer tried to bite President Obama, then fled the theater. Authorities are still hunting for the Obama-nibble showman.

172. Inter Error

I thought he was dead and buried but I was gravely mistaken.

173. Security Team

Exactly how to select qualified personnel to staff an effective security team is a well-guarded secret.

174. Just the Way It Is

You can't make an umlaut without breaking some A's.

175. Foul Mouth Dentist

Dentists are routinely disqualified from
auctions for shouting obscenities.
They're always pulling buy-cuss-bids.

176. Robber E.

Even though the bank robber signed a note with his initials, the police were somehow not able to identify him in their initial investigation.

177. Rice Explosion

I failed at making rice on the stovetop; it exploded onto the walls and ceiling. But if I can collect it, we'll have rice peel-off.

178. Steer Clear

Because the price of beef has skyrocketed, there may be some who can no longer afford to dine at steakhouses. For those of moderate income, it has always been risky to go with friends to a pricey restaurant, but now the steaks are higher.

179. Nail Miracles

Nail technicians make miracles happen. Every day is one man-you-cure after another. That said, your colleagues can be a little pedi.

180. Flag Expert

It wasn't a banner year for the vexillologist, who was forced to retire on account of his flagging health.

181. Doxxing

To refrain from publishing private or identifying information online about your dental irregularities expert is highly un-ortho-doxx.

182. You Know the Drill

The best outcome of a boring job is a hollow victory.

183. Help for Husbands

Have your husband dance with another man sometime to practice following rather than leading, because some men can benefit from a little relationship guy-dance.

184. Hotel Breakfast

"You look very handsome this morning, sir," the hotel server said to me. As it turns out, breakfast was complimentary.

185. Close, But No

I tried taking up two new hobbies at once: knitting, and learning to play Hindustani music. The results were crochet, but no sitar.

186. Favorite Dog

I wish every puppy were a dachshund, but they can't all be wieners.

187. Laugh At Me Will They

Only after dying in obscurity was the comedian's best work released, post-humorously.

188. Street Justice

I knew a tough guy in England who'd beat up anyone for the price of a penny. He didn't care who – but he'd always collect his wreck 'em pence.

189. Wide Receivers

Wide receivers are super competitive. When your rival gets 20 touchdown receptions, you have to match him. But this can be a catch-20 too.

190. Put Your Money Where Your Mouth Is

Brace yourself – this orthodontist isn't going to help you.

191. Veggie Cargo

I wouldn't ship vegetables on ocean-going ships because you don't want a sprig o' leeks.

192. Assembly Required

The "assembly required" furniture came with limited hardware, including just one kind of fastener, which is just plain nuts.

193. Ad Hoc

Hawkman & Hawkgirl don't go on every superhero mission – they're only used on an add-hawk basis.

194. Dessert Cart

After a group has lost their voices singing karaoke is not the time to roll out dessert. That's putting the cart before the hoarse.

195. Hanging Around

I have this big photo of a dictionary, but I don't know where to hang it because I have no frame of reference.

196. Funeral Procession

If the funeral coach breaks down during the procession, don't try going around it, because there's no point beating a dead hearse.

197. Love and War

The theme for this year's Nocturnal Predator Bird Festival is "mating and hunting habits," so owl's fair is love and war.

198. A Penny Saved

Cremated remains are generally kept in copper containers because a penny saved is a penny urned.

199. Try As You Mite

Don't bring up non-monogamous ectoparasite arachnids at dinner, because it can be considered impolite to discuss poly-ticks.

200. Change of Pace

Though I'm stepping down from my role as president of the Driving Club, I do still plan to remain on the Steering Committee.

201. High Strung

Archery is great, but it has its drawbacks.

202. Business Vampires

Vampires make terrible CEOs because they want nothing to do with stakeholders.

203. Shoe Store

The single owner of a shoe store is called a sole proprietor.

204. The Piper

Friends of the balding flutist could no longer avoid the subject. It was time – toupee the piper.

205. Best Playground Equipment

Between Monkey Bars and Trapeze Rings, the title of best playground equipment is up for grabs.

206. Colorful Commentary

Selecting which colors to paint your house is a hues decision.

207. Play Dirt

One can quickly build a house out of grass and turf that looks solid from the outside, but it's all a fast sod.

208. Money Motivation

It's common cents that making money is not a proper motivator for all things. Beware the teachings of false profits.

209. Illusionist Love

When two parlor magicians fall for one another, it's love at first sleight.

210. Freedom of Religion

Everyone's free to decide which branch of which religion they want to subscribe to because our society allows for consensual sects.

211. Another Day

Rooting hair into plastic doll heads is a low paying job, but some appreciate the work. Another day, another doll hair.

212. Bishop's Wordplay

The bishop was actually a great lover of wordplay, as evidenced by his near constant pun-tification.

213. Last Supper

The condemned man was given no proper dinner, as his was just desserts.

214. Bonnet

The DDoS attacker couldn't stop talking about his new honeypot trap. It was the latest bee in his botnet.

215. Hairy Business

Business never wanes in the hair removal industry – it's always waxing.

216. Fighting Fish

I'm working on a video game where you play as a guppy in a tank full of large fighting fish. We're not currently live though, we're still in beta 'testines.

217. Faithful Reproduction

While playing the ancestor of the modern harp, one must frequently check the tuning because you can never trust a lyre.

218. Every Comment Section

Wise guys love trading insults online so much that every comment section on the internet is well e-quipped.

219. Yea, Doughnuts!

We're doing a survey of popular doughnut styles and there's been no negative votes so far. All beignets.

220. NRA Presentation

It's not that the NRA's presentation was bad per se, but their slides had far too many bullet points.

221. Game On!

Every time I hear the kids in the street call out "Car!", wait for it to pass, and then yell "Game on!", I can't help but laugh. It's quite the play-on words!

222. Either

I could really use some chromite or dolomite, either ore.

223. Or

When it comes to kayaking versus canoeing, you have to choose either oar.

224. Steer Clear

The poker legend became a cattle rancher later in life to raise the steaks.

Part Three:

PUNishment

225. Insect Nutrition

Is honey an important source of bee vitamins?

226. Drives Me Crazy

I hate the traffic and gridlock of driving through a city, but the exits are my real turn-offs.

227. Why the Long Face?

Horses make very negative pets, as every single one is a neigh sayer.

228. Alarm Ring Discovery

Sometimes our bell system at school is not working and we just watch the clocks ourselves, stand in the doorway, and shout "Ring, ring!" down the hall. It's an effective solution, and may be innovative enough to earn a no-bell prize.

229. Walk in the Park

If your neighbor to the west has an empty outdoor space you'd like to use, then there's a lot left to be desired.

230. Once in a Lifetime

The employee of a sporting goods store was honored to be asked to lower the price of a basketball on clearance, for she saw it as a re-mark a ball opportunity.

231. Out of Luck

A biology teacher tried several times to bring in newts for dissecting, but each time they arrived too far decomposed. He really needed some good newts for a change.

232. Fair Repair

Two auto body shops were accused of price-fixing after authorities learned that the businesses were collusion specialists.

233. The Truth

My sister is basically an honest person, but she wants to get along with her friend and when they're together they are not always truthful. A peer and sis can be deceiving.

234. Patience

When you're young and starting out, you might not be able to afford many luxuries. But don't worry, as this is just "Sparta life."

235. Flying High

Smugglers accidently left a bale of marijuana on the beach by the Texas gulf. The local birds swarmed the bale and devoured it, leaving no tern unstoned.

236. Foot Lose

The dancer didn't want to tell his choreographer that he had injured his foot and therefore could not be at practice, because it was such a lame excuse.

237. Life's a Beach

The serfs in early communist Russia found life tedious and boring. They didn't work very hard because they had no incentive to do so. One seldom sees any productive work in the vicinity of a serf bored.

238. Water It Be?

Angel Falls in Venezuela is so high that a lot of the water that flows over it evaporates before it reaches the bottom. For a drop of water going over the edge, it's either hit or mist.

239. The Mouth of the Beholder

There was a chewing gum line that was doing research on a new gum flavor. They tried to keep careful statistics on how many subjects purchased the new flavor, but they couldn't get a system that would record the data reliably. It seems that there's no accounting for taste.

240. A Bit of Advice

Be careful feeding the hogs by hand, and remember not to feed the ham that bites you.

241. Safety is Key

I'm always careful when I leave home to make sure that the front gate is securely locked; it's the latch thing I do.

242. Fish Food & Fate

A hatchery in New England was experimenting with a new fish food, but they weren't sure if the fish would eat it. After a week, they dissected a few of the fish to see if they had eaten any, but it just wasn't in the cods.

243. Ready or Not

For special African drums made of goat hide, replacement can mean a whole afternoon devoted to a game of hide and goat seek.

244. Food for Thought

In kindergarten they sometimes do artwork which involves gluing Cheerios onto paper to form an image, otherwise known as Cerealism.

245. Mall? What Mall?

Two friends went to meet their old classmate, Juan, who worked at a clothing store in a shopping center. Afterwards, one of them was referring to the trip to the mall, but the other was not aware that there was a mall, as they were only in the one store. His friend assured him, "When you've seen Juan, you've seen the mall."

246. Cheese Louise

The Army's elite, the Green Berets, get their famous hats from a plant in Oshkosh, WI. The most coveted positions in the plant are those in packaging where they ship the finished berets out to the military. In Wisconsin, nobody is more respected than a green beret packer.

247. Gnome Way Out

The tiny subway system in my garden always runs on time thanks to its mini metro gnomes.

248. Culinary Infidelity?

I offered to make coffee-infused, German-style sausages for my wife, but she warned me that if I did, it would be grounds for *die Wurst*.

249. Sick Burn

I've been told my new sun tan is a-peeling.

250. Sharp Wit

Can I make a cutting joke? Sword of.

251. Sweetness

What's the best Italian dessert? I cannoli guess.

252. Shhh!

In my monastery, speaking is not aloud.

253. Potty Humor

These new self-crapping pants are pretty slick!

254. You Can Take the Boy Outta Iowa

Life on the farm may look interesting, but raising pigs is sow boaring.

255. Cold Feet

Never date a snowman – they're so flaky.

256. Plenty of Invertebrates in the Sea

Never date a sponge – they're so self-absorbed.

257. Too Much Money

I tried to move my money around, but I couldn't budget.

258. The Miracle of Kitten-Birth

Cats give birth to multiple kittens at once: litterly.

259. New Look

I decided to grow my beard out, just a hair.

260. A Half-Baked Bright Idea

I can't get my new Electric Scone recipe to hold a currant.

261. Moo Cow Coup

Evidence of a vegan plot to stop the flow of cow's milk was utterly damming.

262. Holier Than Thou

The priest attributed a shortage of communion wine to demonic spirits, and so exorcised pour judgment.

263. True Forgiveness

I would like whoever stole my body wash to come clean about it.

264. Language of Love

How do deaf lover's communicate?
Sighing language.

265. No Thank You

A dessert that has been left out for too long can be off pudding.

266. Better Under Pressure

It's proving difficult to wall mount my herbs without a thyme frame.

267. Feeling the Crunch

I need numerical data rendered from a sample – *Stat!*

268. Exit Through the Vomitorium

Drinking too much apple beer can lead to an ex-cidering evening.

269. Workplace Drama

The bartender and his foam scraper often found themselves at lager heads.

270. Equine-nimity

Regular grooming and plenty of hay is the key to maintaining a stable relationship.

271. Ancient Insubordination

When Cleopatra instructed an opinionated slave to wave a palm leaf at her, his last words were, "Eh. I'm not a big fan."

272. Shoo-In

Winning the World's Largest Shoe
contest was no small feet.

273. Starting a New Chapter

The first step in upkeeping your library should be to clean the Dickens out of it.

274. Sensible Cooking

What did the concerned sauce say to the overwrought noodles? "Don't strain yourself!"

275. Cut Your Losses

The local shopping center was given away in a raffle, and when I lost I thought, well... you can't win a mall.

276. Fake Bake

If we put stomach varnish to a vote, I'll be ab-staining.

277. Rule of Thumb

When it comes to restaurant reservations, never judge the covers by the book.

278. In the Know

If there's a new development regarding my Permanent Mammary Gland Transformation potion, I'll be sure to keep you a breast.

279. Wintery Mixed Greens

With the right pressure and freezing temperatures, cabbage can actually float up into the clouds. If anything changes, lettuce snow.

280. Supplement My Lifestyle

I'm the best at not being a vitamin – I've never been B10.

281. Hidden Meaning

The illustrator of "Where's Waldo," Martin Handford, sure can draw a crowd!

282. Don't Even Bother

Asking a pothead for a suggestion is refer madness.

283. You Gotta Try This

My new herb seasoning is simply un-bay leaf-able.

284. Favorite Food

I tried asking people which kind of kebab they liked more, but the results of the pole were totally skewered.

285. Art Reflects Life

Like all good poets, iamb what I am.

286. Personal Preference

I prefer to cut my cheese with a knife. I find that, in this case, the grater is lesser.

287. Arch Enemy

Ancient architects took one look at the hemispherical top of that new building and thought, "Well, *that's* dome."

288. Sedimentary School

Learning about wines can be a terroir-ifying experience.

289. Coffin Up, Already

If you want a dignified burial, you've got to urn it.

290. To Thine Own Self, Be You

When my fiancée forgets to sling her purse over her shoulder before we leave, she has failed to purse on-ify herself.

291. Nope

All the people I deny... they just don't get it.

292. Bovine Stationery

I've invented a paper made from a cows teat that erases itself every hour. It's utterly remarkable!

293. Slow-Pork

Tenderizing bacon can be a difficult process, so do them one strip at a time – you don't wanna beat two lardons yourself.

294. Smoke 'Em if You Got 'Em

When do military potheads get excited? 16:20!

295. Higher Authority

No matter how wrecked the keeper of the church can get, remember: they can always get rector.

296. Financial Future

I finally decided to invest in gold. I just hope it was worth the weight....

297. So Much To Do

I'm going to arrange a group Solitaire night for my Introverts Club, but first I need to figure out what to plan for the Procrastinators Anonymous meeting....

298. Look Ma, No Hands!

The prospect of designing human prosthetics based on dog and cat anatomy gives me paws.

299. Swear Like a Sailor

If you think you can talk ship to me, just frigate about it!

300. Reining in Government

Giving deer their own state-backed currency might well create Stag Nation.

301. Meow-vie Night

Why is it so frustrating to watch movies with kitties? They love to press paws.

302. Neutral Party

If you're looking for a side dish that's neither good nor bad when picnicking with the French, come see coleslaw.

303. The Big Reveal

Is the NSA spying on innocent civilians? There's Snowden out about it.

304. Lumberjack

What's a lumberjack's favorite kind of beer? Lager.

305. Biology 101

How do the cells in your body produce
energy? Well, I'm not sure, but you could
try asking Native Americans – one of
them might know how to make ATP.

306. Devil's Advocate

I'm not a big fan of hard-boiled eggs cut
in half and filled with a yolk-mayo-
mustard paste, but I'll play deviled
advocate.

307. Unclear

Maybe you can understand how water
vaporizes and condenses, but I haven't
the foggiest idea.

308. Santa's Standup

You wouldn't expect Santa Claus to be such a funny standup comedian, but he totally sleighs.

309. Sleeping Dogs

If your dog takes a nap right after trying to deceive you, remember it's best not to let sleeping dogs lie.

310. Paper Mill Noir

I wanted to write a novel about a hardboiled PI investigating a paper mill, but since somebody else already did it, I was beaten to a pulp.

311. Cleanliness

Motorcyclists must protect their eyes from projectiles, debris, and splatter, because cleanliness is next to goggley-ness.

312. Windstorm Damage

As there was very little actual property damage, the reports of windstorm were overblown.

313. Balladeer Transportation

Medieval balladeers traveled on primitive bicycles. Silly as it looked, it was considered vulgar to mock their minstrel cycles.

314. Amorous Astronomers

When the astronomers' work turned amorous, the pair misidentified some heavenly bodies. A classic example of star-crossed lovers.

315. Saucey Artist

The avant-garde artist threw savory sauce on his audience with such solemnity, critics praised his performance for its gravy-toss.

316. Making Beer

As someone who's never brewed unfiltered and unpasteurized beer, who am I to cask judgement?

317. Training in Knots

Sailors learn all kinds of boating knots, but do train crews learn any rope work? Freight knot.

319. Line Ignorance

You know you can't leave a long line and expect to come right back to your same spot again. Ignorance is no ex-queues.

318. Tableware

I can't recommend enough the convenience of keeping some tableware at various places outside your home. Satellite dishes are out of this world!

320. Makeup Artist

The makeup artist refused to take my money because he thought I was just paying lip service.

321. Pouring Liquids

Pouring liquids precisely into a narrow-mouthed bottle is hard to do, funnel-ly enough.

322. Uncouth Engineer

The engineer may have been talented with computer-aided drafting, but as for his designs on the ladies, he was a real CAD.

323. Fabulous

Taking the keyfob with you when you park is great, but leaving it inside your vehicle is just plain fob-you-left!

324. Downward Facing Kitten

You're telling me you can teach yoga to a cat?! Now *that's* a stretch.

Part Four:

Pun Runs

325. Janitor Disguise

Sweeping changes will be coming to our janitorial policy after a riding floor scrubber was stolen. Whoever did it made a clean getaway.

326. Tea Brewing

Please leaf tea brewing to the professionals. Sure, you could make it yourself, but there's a steep learning curve.

327. No Sprain, No Gain

Brace yourselves for this twist, but I sprained my ankle pretty badly yesterday. I understand this isn't swell news – in fact it's pretty lame – and I don't want to get off on the wrong foot while we're tendon to work late with so much to do. I don't intend to use this as a crutch or let anyone else foot the bill for my misstep. I promise that you will be able to lean on me soon, and I'll toe the line when it comes time to step up to the task. I wouldn't have a leg to stand on otherwise.

328. Pushing My Buttons

The director of a new show called "QWERTY" texted the press to say that type casting was key to making a hit.

329. Furniture Debate

The Ottoman left everyone floored when he couched his opinion, dropped his counter argument, and tabled the issue. Sofa, so good.

330. Clothing Scandal

The clothier was really hanging by a thread when his lawyer finally saw a pattern in how he was stringing them along. Turns out the whole suit was fabricated, just made up out of whole cloth.

331. Hindsight is 20/20

Bringing in another set of eyes helped to bring everything into focus: in hindsight, the bespectacled man did not actually kill his optometrist. Clearly, he was framed.

332. Too Much Room, or Not Too Much Room

Because these sporesly populated mushrooms are capped by their inherent fungibility, eliminating them entirely would be no truffle at all.

333. Bluffing

Your steep rocky cliff that's mostly flat on top is pretty nice, but ours is a real butte. Even so, I've got a mounting suspicion we're going to plateau somewhere.

334. Casual Office

Even though I thought we were tied, I will bow to your superior neckwear. I know knot why it was a full win, sir.

335. Ointment

I don't mean to rub it in, but making rash decisions about skin treatment options can make you a sore-loser.

336. Angry Doctor

There's a short tempered endocrinologist who specializes in growth hormones. As you might imagine, he has little patients. They seek him out because he's part of the growing medical field.

337. Salt Solutions

Despite making a few salient points, the chemist's ideas about sea water solutions just didn't hold water. And I had been crystal clear when I asked them not to use such salty language, but Na....

338. Gotta Hand It To Ya

I can't put a finger on what I find so sinister about ambidexterity. We'll have to knuckle down, mano a mano, because if I'm right, then my hands are tied.

339. A Vicious Cycle

I spoke too soon: what the re-tired cyclist did was so off the chain that we had to put the brakes on immediately to get a handle on it. Once we were in the right frame of mind, we could change gears and move on. No one wanted to fixie on the un-in-ten-speed consequences.

340. Color Me Shocked

Someone dyed last night and investigators are stumped. It's a real hue done it.

341. Hairy Flocking Sheep

One sheep said, "The shepherd is going to cut off our wool today." "Are you kidding?" asked a second sheep. "Every year they force us into the barn and cut off our wool," said the first. The second cried, "The shear audacity!" Soon the shepherd arrived and started moving the sheep toward the barn. "Stop," cried a sheep. "You're herding me!" Later, after the sheep looked at his new, thinner appearance, his anger started to fade; he was a lot less wool-ful.

342. Neighbor's Yard

Call me paranoid, but I think the gravedigger next door is plotting against us. I know that sort of undertaking constitutes a grave accusation, but if it's true, then we are interring new territory.

343. No Skin Off My Back

Strip away the hairy grand opening and the waxing salon was a rip-roaring success.

344. Cut From a Different Cloth

The only blanket statement I shawl ever make – and I've said this sheet afghan and afghan – is never to quilt while you're ahead.

345. Spice is the Variety of Life

Some sage advice: don't overlook the gift potential of spices. My mother has several sets of herbs, but her favorite is the one I got her for her birthday. After all, there's no thyme like the present.

346-A. Pop Fizz

Have you ever airdropped a case of cola onto a storm front? It's sodas gusting.

346-B. Bottles Up

I could bench press a case of cola, but that would be soda pressing.

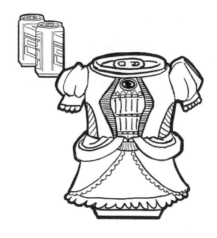

346-C. Can Do

I find children fitting doll clothes onto cans of cola sodas-dressing.

347. Hotdog Master

The hotdog master destroyed his competitors. They tried to play ketchup, but couldn't cut the mustard, and he dispatched them with relish.

348. Hair Today

Choosing to sport a pageboy haircut is a bowled decision that requires planning a head.

349. Gun Lobbyist

Give a gun lobbyist a magazine and he'll shoot through it at a fast clip. Make a request without offering a kickback and he'll recoil.

350. A Bit Gruff

Billy may be a bit sheepish, but he rammed that kid who got his goat. He's on the lamb now, ewe know.

351. Busy Chiropractor

With back to back appointments, the chiropractor was so anxious to get cracking she didn't notice that a private investigator was spine on the joint.

352. Success in Radio

Static-ticians have uncovered how to succeed in radio: tune into your demographic and generate buzz that really resonates with people.

353. Racetrack

After talking so much at the racetrack, my voice is a little horse. Now saddled with gambling debts, I manely regret ponying up.

354. Addicted to Heroines

I'm looking for one of those shoot-em-ups in circulation featuring a strong heroine, or something in a similar vein.

355. Vent Tech

Our ventilation technician has drafted some grate ideas, but he's been known to duct out of work, giving us the shaft.

356. Moist You Go On?

The comedian's rant about creams, ointments, and moisturizers was a pore excuse for topical humor.

357. Dry Humor

A raisinable vendor of dried fruit would be prune-dent to keep up to date on currant affairs. Go fig!

358. Key Results

It really struck a chord with me to learn that while musicians are instrumental to your success, only the singers will be vocal about it.

359. The Candy Man

The confectioner is a sweet guy with refined tastes. But he gives questionable advice, due to his habit of sugarcoating everything.

360. Religion & Horses

You'll find many brainwashed, young, male horses in religious colts. In steed, they'll foal for anything.

361. Alan Turing

I asked Turing if he'd received any robo-calls lately, but he didn't know the first thing a-bot it. Good thing too, he de-tests them.

362. Otterly Preposterous

It's whiskey to let marine mammals get drunk scotch free, so we now have specially trained police units equipped to subdue rye-otters.

363. Doughboy

The Pillsbury Doughboy has no technical aptitude, he was hired for his soft skills. So when the heat is on, he flakes.

364. Principal's Mortgage

The principal's principle interest was in making mortgage payments to principal, not interest.

365. Posh Purse

If you had to carry your standard transmission around in a stylish, tiny little bag, you'd have to clutch a clutch clutch clutch.

About the Authors

Legendary Puns was written by a collection of middle children brothers and their father.

Kevin Kelleher (Bro #4) is an author, composer, gamer, and playwright living in New York City with his wife Laura and their cat, Slinky. He is author of the fantasy adventure series, *Chronicles of Gilderam*, and his plays and musicals are performed regularly around the country.

Learn more at kevinfkelleher.com, follow on Twitter at @kevinfkelleher and Instagram at kev.kelleher

Lucas Kelleher (Bro #3) is a writer, video game designer, and graphic artist living in Seattle, WA with his wife Marissa. His first book, *Shakotan Blue*, is a humorous travel guide and memoir about his time in Japan. He is also editor of kelleherbros.com and creator of most of its content.

Read more at kelleherbros.com, follow on Twitter at @propelleher and Instagram at propelleher

Michael Kelleher (Bro #2) is a father and engineer living in Seattle, WA with his wife Samantha and their children and dog.

Stephen Kelleher is a multi-talented musician specializing in guitar and lute, and a retired teacher from Fort Dodge, Iowa. Stephen is the father of the above-mentioned Kellehers, plus a couple more sons we didn't even have room to include. When it comes down to it, this is really all his fault.